WITHDRAWN

Carmelo Anthony

SUPERSTARS IN THE WORLD OF BASKETBALL

LeBron James

Dwyane Wade

Kobe Bryant

Carmelo Anthony

Kevin Durant

Chris Paul

Dwight Howard

Rajon Rondo

Blake Griffin

Players & the Game Around the World

SUPERSTARS IN THE WORLD OF BASKETBALL

Carmelo Anthony

Aurelia Jackson

Mason Crest

Mason Crest
450 Parkway Drive, Suite D
Broomall, PA 19008
www.masoncrest.com

Printed and bound in the United States of America.

First printing
9 8 7 6 5 4 3 2 1

Series ISBN: 978-1-4222-3101-2
ISBN: 978-1-4222-3103-6
ebook ISBN: 978-1-4222-8793-4

The Library of Congress has cataloged the
hardcopy format(s) as follows:
        Library of Congress Cataloging-in-Publication Data

Jackson, Aurelia.
  Carmelo Anthony / Aurelia Jackson.
      pages cm. — (Superstars in the world of basketball)
  ISBN 978-1-4222-3103-6 (hardback) — ISBN 978-1-4222-3101-2 (series) — ISBN 978-1-4222-8793-4 (ebook) 1. Anthony, Carmelo, 1984—Juvenile literature. 2. Basketball players—United States--Biography--Juvenile literature. I. Title.
  GV884.A58J34 2015
  796.323092—dc23
  [B]
                                    2014005512

Contents

1. Dreams of the NBA   7

2. Getting Better   17

3. Pushing Forward   27

4. NBA All-Star   37

Series Glossary of Key Terms   45

Find Out More   46

Index   47

About the Author & Picture Credits   48

KEY ICONS TO LOOK FOR:

Text-Dependent Questions: These questions send the reader back to the text for more careful attention to the evidence presented there.

Words to Understand: These words with their easy-to-understand definitions will increase the reader's understanding of the text, while building vocabulary skills.

Series Glossary of Key Terms: This back-of-the book glossary contains terminology used throughout this series. Words found here increase the reader's ability to read and comprehend higher-level books and articles in this field.

Research Projects: Readers are pointed toward areas of further inquiry connected to each chapter. Suggestions are provided for projects that encourage deeper research and analysis.

Sidebars: This boxed material within the main text allows readers to build knowledge, gain insights, explore possibilities, and broaden their perspectives by weaving together additional information to provide realistic and holistic perspectives.

Words to Understand

eliminated: Removed from competition after losing.

persevered: Kept going even when it was difficult.

siblings: Brothers or sisters.

role models: People you can look up to.

selective: Picky or choosy (to make sure only the best get in).

statistics: Numbers that show important information (like the total number of points a player scored in a season or how many shots a team missed during a game).

DREAMS OF THE NBA

Carmelo Anthony's shoes squeak as he dashes across the court floor. His teammates aren't far behind. Sweat drips down his face, showing that he is working hard. The entire United States basketball team is tired, but they can't rest just yet. They have an international championship to win, and this is one of the first games of the series.

Carmelo dribbles the ball to the three-point line and takes a second to line up his shot. Then he jumps . . . shoots . . . and scores!

For a player to make a basket from the three-point line, he must have great aim. Carmelo is known for his ability to make a basket from anywhere on the court. It helped him score many more points that day.

In fact, on August 2, 2012, Carmelo Anthony made history by scoring 37 points in a single Olympic basketball game. He is the first and only Olympic athlete to do this.

The team Carmelo and the rest of the U.S. team were facing was Nigeria. In the end, the United States beat the Nigerian team by scoring a total of 156 points. Nigeria only

Carmelo was born in Brooklyn, New York. Things weren't always easy for Carmelo and his family living in Brooklyn. The family didn't have much money and would have to move to Baltimore, Maryland, while Carmelo was still very young.

scored 73. This was the third team the United States had faced in the 2012 Olympic Games. After the game, Nigeria was *eliminated*, and the United States moved on to the next round. The U.S. basketball team went on to earn the gold medal for its second Olympics in a row. Carmelo had been part of the team back in 2008 as well.

After earning his Olympic medal, Carmelo was asked how it felt to win gold for a second time in a row. He said, "It's unexplainable. All our hard work has paid off since we started back in Vegas."

The U.S. basketball team is made up of players from all over the country. These athletes do not normally play together. They need to train a lot to learn how to work well together on the court. Becoming the best team in the world is never easy. Every teammate needs to play his best.

"We knew it wasn't going to be easy," Carmelo added. "We stuck together and we *persevered*."

The interviewer also asked Carmelo what the medal meant for the United States. He said, "I hope it means a lot. I hope it means everything. Our country is behind us. Our fans are behind us. We came over here and we did this for then. I'm proud of everybody."

Olympic basketball players from the United States do not get paid to compete. When they take part in the Olympics, they do it for free. For Carmelo, the honor of earning an Olympic gold medal is better than any paycheck.

It had been a long road that brought him to this moment. He had worked hard to get to the Olympics. But for Carmelo, every inch of his journey was worth it!

GROWING UP

Carmelo Kyam Anthony was born on May 29, 1984, in Brooklyn, New York. (Brooklyn is one of New York City's five sections, or boroughs.) Carmelo was named after his father, who came from a Puerto Rican family. His mother, Mary, is African-American. Carmelo never really got to know his father, because he died of cancer when Carmelo was just two years old.

The death of Carmelo's father left Mary alone to raise her young child, as well as her other three children. She worked as a housekeeper to make ends meet. (Housekeepers are paid to clean and manage the households of other people.) Being a single mother was not easy for Mary. She needed to work very long hours to earn enough money to support the family.

While she was at work, her older children took care of Carmelo. They helped raise him. This is when Carmelo started to love basketball. He watched basketball games on television. He looked forward to the NBA playoffs every year.

When Carmelo was eight years old, his older *siblings* were ready to move out and live on their own. This left Carmelo and his mother to fend for themselves. Without the help of her other children, Mary had a hard time finding the money to put food on the

After moving to Baltimore, Carmelo went to high school in a town outside of Baltimore named Towson. There, Carmelo attended the Catholic high school, where he'd learn to love basketball even more than he had as a child.

Like many famous basketball players, Carmelo tried out a lot of different sports when he was young. He liked pitching in baseball, and he was a receiver in football. Of all the sports he played, though, Carmelo liked basketball the best. By the time Carmelo tried out for the varsity team in high school, he was putting all of his energy into basketball.

table. Carmelo was left on his own a lot, because his mother was working so much of the time.

Mary knew that she and her youngest son could not stay in Brooklyn if they wanted to survive. They needed to move to a place where it didn't cost so much to live. Mary chose Baltimore, Maryland, to be their new home. This city is about four hours away from New York City.

Carmelo and his mother moved into a Baltimore neighborhood known as "The Pharmacy." Living in this neighborhood had its ups and downs. On the one hand, it was easy to afford. Mary could pay the bills and take care of Carmelo without needing to leave him alone too much. However, this neighborhood was also very dangerous. The streets were filled with crime and illegal drugs. It was not the best place to raise a child, but Mary had no choice. She was doing the best that she could alone.

Children who grow up in bad neighborhoods can get caught up in doing illegal things. Without good *role models*, they might become drug dealers or gang members later in life. Criminals who are caught go to prison for a long time. If Mary wasn't careful, Carmelo could fall into this lifestyle. She was determined not to let that happen.

One of the things that kept Carmelo out of trouble as a kid was basketball. Watching the sport on TV was no longer enough for him. Carmelo began playing basketball while he was growing up in Baltimore. His mother used his love for basketball to keep him in line. She told Carmelo that if he ever got bad grades in school, she wouldn't let him play basketball. This plan worked. Being able to play basketball on the court was Carmelo's reward for doing well in school.

STARTING SLOW

Mary worked hard for many years to make sure Carmelo was able to get a good education. If he were going to get better at basketball, he needed to go to a great high school. This is why she sent him to a high school in a different neighborhood from where they

Long before he was playing here in the world-famous Madison Square Garden, Carmelo was just another high school basketball fan, working on his jump shot and trying to make the varsity team.

CARMELO ANTHONY

Research Project

Using the Internet or by visiting your local library, find out more information about the position of point guard. What does the point guard do to help the team? How does the point guard work with the other players? Where on the court does the point guard play most often? What is the point guard's job when the team is on defense? On offense? Who are some of the most famous point guards in the NBA today? Who are some of the most famous point guards who have played the game in the past?

lived. He began attending Towson Catholic High School in 1998. It was a forty-five-minute drive away from his house. To Carmelo and his mother, the travel time was worth it.

Carmelo was eager to show off his skills when he first entered high school. He tried out for the varsity team. Varsity teams are very *selective*. This means that the team only takes the best players. Carmelo showed real promise on the court, though, and he was picked to join the team.

Carmelo's first position in high school was as a point guard. Point guards are known for their ball handling and passing skills. Carmelo was very good at this position.

Carmelo was a skilled player. However, his coach didn't think he was ready to play against other high school students. Carmelo wasn't tall, and he wasn't muscular. His team-mates were also more experienced than Carmelo was. All varsity basketball players are also high school students. These students are usually between the ages of thirteen and eighteen. That's a very big age gap for growing boys! It is possible for high school seniors to be over a foot taller than freshman. At the time, Carmelo was fourteen, and he just wasn't big enough to compete on a varsity team. He was cut from the team during his first year.

But everything changed during the summer before Carmelo's second year of high school. He grew a lot. By the start of his sophomore year, Carmelo was six feet and five inches tall. This may seem very tall compared to most humans, but it is actually an average height for American basketball players! Carmelo had spent the year working hard to improve his skills and it certainly showed.

He was brought back onto the varsity team. This time, he did very well as a small forward and a shooting guard. Shooting guards are great at shooting baskets, while small forwards need to be quick on their feet. A person who can play both of these positions is known as a swingman.

Carmelo began to make a name for himself during his sophomore year. He averaged

They may be young, but many high school students are already great basketball players. For a few players, high school basketball is just the beginning of a long career playing the sport. Here, high school player Amar Stukes leaps for the basket during a game in Philadelphia.

Text-Dependent Questions

1. How did the U.S. basketball team do in the 2012 Olympics?

2. Describe Carmelo and Mary's life after moving to Baltimore.

3. How did Carmelo's mom use basketball to push Carmelo to do well in school?

4. What was Carmelo's first year in high school basketball like?

5. What changed for Carmelo for his second season of high school basketball?

14 points, 5 rebounds, 4 assists, and 2 steals per game. Those *statistics* are great for a new player! With Carmelo's help, the Towson Catholic High School team was able to finish third in the state tournament. This year was only the beginning of his very successful high school career. Over the next two years, Carmelo would continue to get better. His coach also started giving him a lot more time on the court.

Words to Understand

professional: Paid to play.
options: Choices.
adjust: To get used to something.
exception: Something or someone that is different from what's normal or doesn't follow the same pattern or rule as everyone else.
press conference: A meeting with reporters meant to get a message out to the people.

GETTING BETTER

Carmelo's high school career began to soar in his junior year. His average points per game nearly doubled from what they had been during his last season. The rest of the state began to notice how talented he was. Towson Catholic was not able to win the state championship, but Carmelo did win a few awards of his own. He was named the Baltimore City and County Player of the Year. He also became the All-Metropolitan and Baltimore Catholic League Player of the Year.

By the time Carmelo reached his senior year, he needed to start thinking about his future. Would he play in a college league—or did he want to try to join the NBA? Carmelo's dream was to join the NBA, but he just wasn't ready yet. He was skilled but still very thin. **Professional** basketball players need to be big and strong. They train almost every day to stay in shape. Carmelo was tall enough to join the NBA, but he didn't have the strength. NBA scouts did not care about Carmelo while he was still in high school because he didn't have the right build yet. So Carmelo decided to go to college first. Going to college would give Carmelo time to get stronger and improve his skills even more.

NBA star Ty Lawson also went to Oak Hill Academy to play basketball. Later, Ty went on to play for the Denver Nuggets just like Carmelo.

Make Connections

The National Basketball Association (NBA) is the most important men's professional basketball league in North America and in the world. It has thirty member teams (twenty-nine in the United States and one in Canada). NBA players are the world's highest-paid sportsmen (by average annual salary per player).

Carmelo announced that he was planning to attend Syracuse University before his senior year even started. He wanted to train at that college because he liked the head coach of the Syracuse team. Getting into that school wouldn't be easy, though. Carmelo needed to have good grades and great test scores to be accepted into the college. At the time, his high school grades were not good. He had a C average and low scores on his ACT. (The ACT is a type of test that many students take when applying to college.) If Carmelo was going to get into Syracuse University, he needed to improve his grades quickly!

Thanks to his skills on the court, Carmelo had become very popular throughout his high school career. All famous athletes need to learn to deal with this attention. At first, for Carmelo, it was too much to handle. His reputation started going to his head. His grades began to suffer as a result. He was even suspended from school a few times because he stopped going to class. (A suspended student is not allowed to come to school for a certain amount of time. This includes playing sports for the school.) It took some time, but Carmelo was able to get used to his new life. He stopped skipping class, and he focused on his game. During Carmelo's senior year, he started getting better grades, too. He knew there was a lot at stake.

Being able to get into a good college was important to Carmelo. He decided to go to a different high school to finish his senior year. Carmelo and his mother hoped going to a new school would help him focus on getting better both in the classroom and on the court. They looked at a bunch of different schools. In the end, Carmelo chose to go to Oak Hill Academy. The basketball team there had won the *USA Today* high school championship in 2001, making it a great fit for a player like Carmelo Anthony.

Joining the Oak Hill high school team was a great decision. Carmelo took summer classes to improve his English and math skills. At the same time, he continued practicing on the court and working out in his free time. Between his junior and senior year, Carmelo became very muscular. He had grown to his full height of six feet and eight inches. He was finally ready to take on even the toughest of opponents.

The Oak Hill Warriors did very well after Carmelo joined. The team won several tournaments including the Nike Academy National Invitational. That year, the Warriors won sixty-seven games in a row before losing to another team. Carmelo made a name for himself during a few different All-Star Games. He scored 27 points during the Michal Jordan's

Carmelo's new life at Syracuse University was very different from his childhood in New York and his time in Baltimore. Syracuse is a big sports school, with popular basketball and football teams. In this picture, you can see the white top of the famous Carrier Dome, where football games are held.

Brand Capitol Classic and 19 points in the McDonald's All-American game. To top it all off, Hoop Scoop named him the best senior high school player of that year.

At the start of Carmelo's senior year, he planned to go to college. During the school year, he worked very hard to be able to make it into college. By the end of that same year, Carmelo's **options** changed, though. He was now a famous high school basketball player. NBA scouts were watching Carmelo, and now they believed he could get into the NBA straight out of high school. Carmelo wasn't sure what to do, so he took the college entrance exam. If his score were high enough, he would go to college. Carmelo scored a nineteen on his ACT. This was more than enough to get into Syracuse University. He started getting ready to leave for college that fall.

SYRACUSE UNIVERSITY

In 2002, Carmelo packed his bags and moved to upstate New York. Unlike Baltimore, Syracuse can be very cold during the fall and winter months. The school was also far away from Carmelo's home. He had some trouble getting used to living there. Finding his classes was hard because he didn't know the area. One place where Carmelo felt right at home, though, was on the basketball court. Before Carmelo even arrived, many of the

Syracuse University's men's basketball team coach Jim Boheim has been coaching basketball at the school for more than 30 years. Under his coaching, Syracuse has become one of the best teams in college basketball. He coached Carmelo during his season with Syracuse.

students at his new school couldn't wait to meet him. The school's basketball coach was excited to see Carmelo play for the Syracuse Orangemen.

Carmelo wasted no time showing his fans what he could do. He had a great year as a freshman. The Orangemen made it to the finals of the national tournament and won! Carmelo scored 20 points and 10 rebounds in the final game. This earned him the title of Most Outstanding Player for that year. At the end of the season, Carmelo averaged about 22 points per game. His average was much higher than other freshmen in the league.

Carmelo originally planned to stay at Syracuse University for at least two or three years. He was going to use this time to improve his game and increase his chances of getting into the NBA. When freshmen join a college basketball team, they usually don't do as well as Carmelo did. They need a lot of time to **adjust** to living on a college campus and competing in a college league. Carmelo was an **exception**. It was easy for him to do well playing basketball because he had been practicing his whole life. He even earned the title of Freshman of the Year for the Big East Conference.

By the end of Carmelo's freshman year, he had done everything he wanted to do. He felt there was nothing left to accomplish at the college level. Even Carmelo's coach agreed that Carmelo was ready to move on. That year, Carmelo announced that he would be signing himself up for the 2003 NBA draft. He wanted to see how far he could get in the national basketball world.

The choice to leave Syracuse was a difficult one. Carmelo had learned a lot from his coach and his fellow teammates. During the **press conference** where Carmelo announced he would be leaving, he cried several times. It was a very emotional moment, but Carmelo knew he needed to move on if he wanted to get better. It was clear by this point that he would be a top pick in the NBA draft.

THE NBA DRAFT

After a player signs up for the NBA draft, he has to wait until a special day to be chosen. The draft is an official event that happens in June every year. All NBA teams take turns

Drafted in the same year as Carmelo (2003), LeBron James has gone on to become one of the biggest stars in the NBA. Like Carmelo, LeBron worked for a spot in the NBA for years, ever since his childhood love of basketball.

Text-Dependent Questions

1. In the last couple years of high school basketball, how well did Carmelo play?

2. What were some of the highlights of Carmelo's time at Oak Hill Academy?

3. How did Carmelo work to get into Syracuse University? Why was the school his first choice?

4. Describe Carmelo's time playing with the Syracuse basketball team.

5. How did the 2003 NBA draft work out for Carmelo?

picking new team members during the draft. The teams that did not do well the year before get to pick first. This is done so that one team does not have an unfair advantage over another one. The NBA draft is meant to make the teams as evenly matched as possible. This way, the NBA tournament is as fair as it can be each year.

The team that gets first pick will usually want to choose the athlete with the best statistics to join the team. The first pick of the 2003 Draft was LeBron James for the Cleveland Cavaliers. Like Carmelo, LeBron was a well-known athlete. The two players had met in 2001 during a competition. The second pick was Darko Miličić for the Detroit Pistons. He was a great ball player from Serbia. Of all the athletes in the draft, Carmelo was picked third overall for the Denver Nuggets. Many players enter the NBA draft each year, so getting picked third is very good!

Carmelo was excited to start his new career as an official NBA player. However, he would have to get used to living in a new city before the season began. The Denver Nuggets are from Colorado. The city of Denver is more than a mile above sea level. It can get extremely cold during the winter, and the air is very thin. Colorado is over a thousand miles away from Carmelo's hometown of Baltimore, Maryland. To practice with the Nuggets, he would need to leave his family behind and get used to his new life in a faraway city in the western United States. It would be hard, but this is what NBA players must deal with when they join the draft.

Carmelo played his first NBA game in October 2003, three short months after he was drafted onto the Denver Nuggets. By this point, he was already used to the NBA training schedule. He had grown much stronger. He was ready to compete against other professionals in the NBA.

Words to Understand

aggressive: Ready to go against others in a tough way.
offensive: Attacking against the other team's basket, trying to score points.
original: First version of something.
milestone: A marker of time passing or a marker of something important happening.
renew: Sign up again for something.
contract: A written agreement between two people or between a person and an organization.
fouled: To be hurt by another player or touched in a way that is against the rules.

PUSHING FORWARD

The Denver Nuggets weren't doing very well before Carmelo joined. The team had won only seventeen games in the last season. This is why Denver was given the third pick in the NBA Draft.

Carmelo was just the type of player the team needed in order to do better. He was young, energetic, and very *aggressive* on the court. This made him a great *offensive* player. The Nuggets hoped that Carmelo would be able to score more points for the team.

It didn't take long for the coach of the Denver Nuggets to figure out that drafting Carmelo was a good choice. During his first game, Carmelo scored 12 points and 7 rebounds. In his sixth game, he scored a total of 30 points. This made him the second youngest player to score that many points in an NBA game. He was just nineteen years old at the time. The only other basketball player in history to score that many points at a younger age was Kobe Bryant.

By February, Carmelo had scored a total of 1,000 points in the NBA. He was the

The Nuggets stadium, the Pepsi Center in Denver, Colorado.

third-youngest player to ever do so. Carmelo had trained his whole life to get ready to play in the NBA. Now that he finally had the chance, he was getting everyone's attention!

Carmelo usually scored a lot of points during any game in which he played. In March of 2004, Carmelo scored 41 points in a game against the Seattle SuperSonics. He was the first rookie of the Denver Nuggets to score this many points in a single game. That same day, he also became the second-youngest player in the NBA to ever score over 40 points during one game. Over the course of Carmelo's career, he would break a lot of records like this.

In the spring of 2004, everyone could tell that Carmelo was easily one of the best rookies in the NBA. He was given the Rookie of the Month award for the first time in April, and he received the award several more times that year. He was also named the NBA Player of the Week twice, once in March and once in April.

At the end of the year, Carmelo was in the running for the Rookie of the Year Award. It is only given to one new player every year, so it is very hard to get. Unfortunately, Carmelo did not win. Instead, the award was given to LeBron James. Carmelo came in second place. He was not disappointed by the loss, though, because he was named to the NBA All-Rookie First Team. Head coaches of the NBA vote on who will be placed on the team.

Carmelo and his teammates worked hard to win games. During the 2003–2004 season, the Denver Nuggets won forty-three games and lost thirty-nine. This was very different from the previous season! The team's wins had doubled in just one year. Carmelo was clearly part of the reason why the Nuggets were doing so well. The year ended when the Nuggets were able to reach the playoffs, but they did not win. Carmelo did what he could, though. In one playoff game, he scored 20 points, 10 rebounds, and 5 assists.

AN OLYMPIC ATHLETE

Carmelo was asked to join the United States Olympic Basketball team after only one year in the NBA. He wasn't part of the *original* team, but a few members had dropped out. This made room for Carmelo. He was eager to take the spot.

Many famous basketball players were a part of the 2004 Olympic Team that competed in Athens, Greece. Some of the most well known were LeBron James and Kobe Bryant. The team played well, and they took home a bronze medal. They'd be going back to the Olympics, and they'd get a chance then to do even better then!

Competing in the Olympics and winning a medal was a great experience for Carmelo, but he was not happy about his time on the court. He didn't get to play very often during the games. Part of the reason was because he was so young compared with the other players. Back home, Carmelo was used to being treated like a star. Overseas, he was just another player. He didn't like warming the bench while his teammates had all the fun.

Carmelo complained to his coaches about not getting much playtime during the Olympic games. He wasn't very quiet about it, and it made news headlines back home. Many

Carmelo dunks the ball during a practice game for the 2012 Olympics.

Make Connections

In the game of basketball, every shot counts. Sometimes, a shot needs to be made at the very end of the game to score the game-winning point. Carmelo became well known for his ability to make jump shots during the last few seconds of a game during the 2005–2006 season. In fact, he won several games this way! A jump shot is a special way of shooting where the player jumps up and throws the ball toward the basket from far away. It is hard for an opponent to stop a jump shot if he can't reach the ball in time.

Nuggets fans were not happy about Carmelo's attitude. This taught Carmelo an important lesson: no matter how popular or successful he becomes, he has to have a good attitude about the game. He has to be thankful for any role he gets, even if he doesn't get to play very often.

Over the next four years, Carmelo improved his attitude. Later, he would be invited back onto the Olympic team two more times, in 2008 and 2012—and he was able to help the United States bring home the gold this time!

GOING AFTER THE FINALS

During the 2004–2005 season, the Denver Nuggets continued to improve. The team won more games that year, with forty-nine victories and thirty-three losses. Carmelo and his teammates finished seventh in the Western Conference. That was one spot higher than the year before. They were slowly getting better, but the Nuggets still had a long way to go.

The 2005–2006 season was a huge **milestone** for both Carmelo and the Denver Nuggets. The team managed to win the Northwest Division, but they lost in the playoffs for the Western Division. Carmelo scored his five thousandth point that year. His average points per game increased to 26.

The Denver Nuggets weren't winning championships, but they were certainly getting better. Carmelo decided to **renew** his **contract** with the Nuggets. He would earn $80 million—not bad for someone who was only twenty-two years old!

During the 2006–2007 season, Carmelo made a big mistake, though. In December of that season, a fight broke out between members of the Denver Nuggets and the New York Knicks. It happened during the last few minutes of the game. Mardy Collins from the Knicks clearly **fouled** J. R. Smith of the Nuggets. The members of the Nuggets were mad, and every player on the court began to fight. The entire fight was caught on camera. Carmelo got mixed up in the violence and punched Mardy Collins in the face.

Referees watch for fouls, stop fights, and make sure players follow the rules of the game. Besides the players and coaches, referees are some of the most important people working in basketball.

During sports, fouls sometimes happen. Fouls are anything that is not allowed during a game. Sometimes, fouls are accidental. At other times, they are on purpose. Tripping or pushing another teammate is considered a foul. Players who commit a foul are punished. Usually, they have to sit out for a certain amount of time from that game, but if the foul is really bad, the player may be suspended from other games, too.

Basketball games can get pretty heated, but hurting another player is never allowed. Every player involved in the brawl was suspended for a certain amount of games. Carmelo received the worst punishment. He was not allowed to play for fifteen games, and he lost more than $600,000 from his salary. Many of Carmelo's fans were disappointed in him. He was the star player of the Denver Nuggets, and the fans felt he should have stayed out of the brawl.

After Carmelo was allowed to return to the court, though, he had a great year. In February, he scored his first career triple-double with 31 points, 10 rebounds, and 10 assists. A triple-double happens when a basketball player scores double digits in any of the five categories of basketball. In Carmelo's case, it was points, rebounds, and assists. That year, Carmelo was named to the Western Conference All-Star Team for the first time. He was the first Nugget to become an All-Star since 2001.

The Denver Nuggets reached the playoffs once again in 2007. Unfortunately, history repeated itself. They lost to the same team they had lost the playoffs to in 2005. The San Antonio Spurs defeated the Nuggets. Carmelo and his team were eliminated.

Research Project

The Denver Nuggets have had some amazing players on the team. Go online to find out more about the legends of the Nuggets. Other than Carmelo, who are some the team's best players, in the past or today? In the past, how did star players help the team's win-loss record? Look up the seasons in which star players were on the Nuggets to learn more about the team's past statistics. Which star Nuggets players did Carmelo get to share the court with during his time with the team?

Moving to the Knicks would be a big change for Carmelo, but he'd soon become one of the team's biggest stars, drawing both fans and a lot of attention.

34   CARMELO ANTHONY

Text-Dependent Questions

1. How did Carmelo's rookie year go?

2. During the 2004 Olympics, what did Carmelo learn about attitude?

3. What happened after Carmelo got involved in the fight during the 2006-2007 season?

4. Why did Carmelo want to leave the Nuggets?

In the next season, Carmelo pushed even harder for a national title. The Nuggets reached the playoffs easily and made it to the Western Conference finals. This was the first time they had done this since Carmelo joined the team. They lost to the Los Angeles Lakers, though, a team that went on to win the NBA Finals.

The 2010–2011 season was Carmelo's eighth year playing with the Nuggets. By this point, he was getting impatient. Carmelo knew he could go further in the basketball world. The Nuggets were holding him back. In all the years Carmelo had been a part of the team, Denver had not once made it to the NBA Finals. His teammates were getting better, but not fast enough for Carmelo. When he was offered another contract to stay with the Nuggets, Carmelo said no. Instead, he requested a trade.

In the NBA, players can be traded from one team to another. Sometimes, a very good player is traded for a few less-talented players. In February of 2011, Carmelo got his wish when he was traded away to the New York Knicks. This was his first choice and favorite team. He was excited to see how far the team could go.

Being a part of the Knicks was the best possible scenario for Carmelo. He had spent the first few years of his life in New York City. The Knicks were his favorite team while he was growing up. By joining the team, he would be able to move back to the city where he had lived as a child. No longer would he have to live in the Denver. Instead, he could practice in New York City, which was a lot closer to his friends and family.

Words to Understand

resigned: Quit.
donate: To give without being paid (usually money, food, or clothing).
charity: Organizations that work to help people in need.
hosts: Puts on or organizes and runs.

NBA All-Star

When Carmelo joined the Knicks, he switched from the number 15 to the number 7. He joined the team in the middle of the season, and he had very little time to get used to playing with new teammates. Fortunately, Chauncey Billups of the Denver Nuggets was traded to the New York Knicks at the same time Carmelo was. They had played together before, and they knew how to work together on the court.

Late in the season, though, Chauncey hurt himself and was unable to play. This forced the rest of the team to take on the playoffs alone.

Chauncey wasn't the only person who injured himself that year. Another teammate, Amar'e Stoudemire, was also unable to play. Amar'e was the star of the Knicks before Carmelo joined. Losing him meant the team would not be at its best when the Knicks went to the Eastern Conference Playoffs. The Knicks lost in the first series of games against the Boston Celtics. Carmelo had joined in the middle of the season, so he tried not to let the loss get him down. Perhaps the next year would be better.

The 2011–2012 season saw a few more changes. The Knicks' coach *resigned* and a new coach took over. His name was Mike Woodson. Thanks to Mike, the Knicks started

Carmelo's time with the Knicks has been filled with excitement. Carmelo and the Knicks haven't won a championship together, but the team is working hard to reach that goal each season.

Make Connections

Earning the title of NBA champion is hard enough. Becoming an international champion is even more difficult. Carmelo began competing in international championships before he was even an adult. He took part in the FIBA Americas Under Eighteen Championship in 2002 and brought home a bronze medal.

Carmelo was first asked to play for the United States in the Olympics in 2004, where he brought home a bronze medal. Two years later, Carmelo competed in the FIBA World Championship and took home a bronze yet again. His first international gold came in 2007 when he played in the FIBA Americas Championship. Carmelo's first Olympic gold medal was in 2008 during the summer games in Beijing. His second was four years later in London.

Throughout his career, Carmelo has been an NBA All-Star a total of six times. NBA All-Stars are voted on by fans to compete in an NBA All-Star game. The two NBA All-Star teams are divided into players from the Eastern Conference and the Western Conference. Carmelo has competed in the All-Star games in 2007, 2008, 2010, 2011, 2012, and 2013. The first few times, he was a part of the Western Conference because he played for the Denver Nuggets. Carmelo became part of the Eastern Conference after he was traded to the Knicks.

Each year, the NBA player with the most scores for the season is named the scoring champion. In the 2012–2013 season, Carmelo Anthony became the scoring champion for the first time. He scored a total of 1,920 points throughout the year and averaged about 28 points per game.

doing better. He changed the team's strategies to match the players on the team. That year, the Knicks team won eighteen games and lost only six. This was a huge improvement over the eighteen wins and twenty-four losses of the season before.

The odds were still against the Knicks in 2012. Five players were injured or sick at some point during the playoffs. Carmelo and the other teammates did their best to carry the team. The Knicks were able to snag one small victory by winning their first game in the playoffs since 2001. They were eliminated after five games, but the Knicks remained positive. Carmelo and Mike Woodson had proved that the team was improving and was only going to get better.

In the 2012–2013 season, the Knicks made it to the finals again. They even managed to win their first series of games against the Boston Celtics. During the series, Carmelo averaged more than 29 points per game.

The victory was short-lived, though. In the next series of games, the Knicks lost against the Indiana Pacers. Carmelo and the rest of the Knicks hoped to do better the next year,

Carmelo married Alani "La La" Vazquez in 2010 after getting engaged in 2004. The couple's wedding was even made into a reality TV show called *LaLa's Full Court Wedding*. Today, *LaLa's Full Court Life* follows Carmelo and LaLa's life together.

though. "I actually see this team being better than last year," Carmelo said in an interview. "That's just my opinion, that's the way we feel. And if we feel that way as a unit, then there's nothing that can come between us."

PERSONAL LIFE

Carmelo has two brothers, one sister, and one half-sister. His brothers are Robert and Wilford. His sister, Michelle, died in 2010. His half-sister is named Daphne.

When Carmelo was just nineteen, he asked his girlfriend, Alani "La La" Vazquez, to marry him. He proposed on Christmas Eve in 2004—and she said yes. Like Carmelo, La La is very popular. She has worked as an actress, a DJ, and a VJ for MTV's *Total Request Live*. On March 7, 2007, La La and Carmelo had a baby boy. They named him Kiyan Carmelo Anthony.

Carmelo currently lives in the Upper West Side of Manhattan in New York City. (Before that, he lived in Denver.) Living in New York gives him a lot of time to see his family and friends even during his busy practicing schedule.

When Carmelo travels, he brings his family with him. His son, Kiyan, went to London with Carmelo when Carmelo competed in the 2012 Olympic Games. On the days Carmelo wasn't competing, he brought Kiyan around London to see the sights.

Carmelo's friends are important to him too. In 2003, plenty of great players joined the NBA draft along with Carmelo. One of those players was LeBron James. Carmelo and LeBron are now very close friends. They chat all the time and have played together on All-Star and Olympic teams.

Like Carmelo, LeBron always wanted to win an NBA championship. He worked very hard to get there. LeBron and the Miami Heat finally managed to win the NBA Finals in 2012. Carmelo was asked in an interview how he felt about it. He said, "I support him 100 percent. I'm actually happy for him—like excited for him—just because of all the things he's been through and things that have been said about him. For him and Miami to finally get there, this is their time right now." Carmelo is a good friend.

Carmelo and his family celebrate Madame Tussaud's Wax Museum's new wax figure of Carmelo. Madame Tussaud's only makes wax figures of the most famous people in the world, and now the collection includes Carmelo.

GIVING TO CHARITY

Professional basketball players make a lot of money. Carmelo is no different. In the 2012-2013 season, he made a total of $23 million. He is one of the highest-paid members of the team. (Only Amar'e Stoudemire makes more than he does.) Many basketball players *donate* at least some of the money they earn to *charity*, and so does Carmelo. He is very thankful for everything he has been given in life. He wants to give back in any way he can.

Playing for the Orangemen jumpstarted Carmelo's career as a professional basketball player—and Carmelo is grateful. After he joined the NBA, he began making more money than he knew what to do with. He decided to give some of that money to the team that started it all. The money he donated to Syracuse University was used to build a new basketball practice area. He hoped this would help the Orangemen improve their skills and do better in future games. The building was dedicated in 2009. Carmelo was even there to make the first shot on the court! This special building is named the Carmelo K. Anthony Practice Facility. It cost more than $3 million to build.

Text-Dependent Questions

1. Why are the numbers 7 and 15 important in Carmelo's life?

2. What role did Chauncey Billups play in Carmelo's first season with the Knicks?

3. How long has Carmelo known La La?

4. How does Carmelo share his success with people in need?

Another area of the world that is important to Carmelo is Baltimore. He grew up in one of the poorest neighborhoods in that city. He knows what it's like to not have a lot of money. This is why he opened the Carmelo Anthony Youth Development Center.

He also **hosts** charity events and donates large amounts of money to natural disaster relief. Over the years, Carmelo has given several million of dollars in cash donations. He was listed as number eight in "The Giving Back 30 List of Largest Charitable Donations by Celebrities in 2006."

Carmelo still has a lot to do, both in his career and in his personal life—and he doesn't play to stop anytime soon. He hasn't met all his goals yet. He'll keep working hard until he does.

Series Glossary of Key Terms

All-Star games: A game where the best players in the league form two teams and play each other.

Assist: A pass that leads to scoring points. The player who passes the ball before the other scores a basket gets the assist.

Center: A player, normally the tallest on the team, who tries to score close to the basket and defend against the other team's offense using his size.

Championship: A set of games between the two top teams in the NBA to see who is the best.

Court: The wooden or concrete surface where basketball is played. In the NBA, courts are 94 feet by 50 feet.

Defensive: Working to keep the other team from scoring points.

Draft (noun): The way NBA teams pick players from college or high school teams.

Foul: A move against another player that is against the rules, mostly involving a player touching another in a way that is not fair play.

Jump shot: A shot made from far from the basket (rather than under the basket) while the player is in the air.

Offensive: Working to score points against the other team.

Playoffs: Games at the end of the NBA season between the top teams in the league, ending in the finals, in which the two top teams play each other.

Point guard: The player leading the team's offense, scoring points and setting up other players to score.

Power forward: A player who can both get in close to the basket and shoot from further away. On defense, power forwards defend against both close and far shots.

Rebound: Getting the ball back after a missed shot.

Rookie: A player in his first year in the NBA.

Scouts: People who search for new basketball players in high school or college who might one day play in the NBA.

Shooting guard: A player whose job is to take shots from far away from the basket. The shooting guard is usually the team's best long-range shooter.

Small forwards: Players whose main job is to score points close to the basket, working with the other players on the team's offense.

Steal: Take the ball from a player on the other team.

Tournament: A series of games between different teams in which the winning teams move on to play other winning teams and losing teams drop out of the competition.

Find Out More

ONLINE

Carmelo Anthony (carmeloanthony) on Twitter
twitter.com/carmeloanthony

Carmelo Anthony Stats, News, Videos, Highlights, Pictures, Bio
espn.go.com/nba/player/_/id/1975

Carmelo Anthony Stats, Video, Bio, Profile | NBA.com
www.nba.com/playerfile/carmelo_anthony

Official Website of Carmelo Anthony
www.thisismelo.com

IN BOOKS

Anthony, Carmelo. *Carmelo Anthony: It's Just the Beginning.* Kirkland, Wash.: Positively for Kids, 2004.

Fishman, Jon M. *Carmelo Anthony (Amazing Athletes).* Minneapolis, Minn.: Lerner Publishing Group, 2013.

Hoblin, Paul. *Carmelo Anthony (Playmakers).* New York: Abdo Publishing Company, 2012.

MacRae, Sloan. *Carmelo Anthony (Sports Heroes).* New York: Powerkids, 2012.

Torsiello, David P. *Read About Carmelo Anthony (I Like Sports Stars!).* Berkeley Heights, N.J.: Enslow Elementary, 2011.

Index

Alani "La La" Vazquez 40–41, 44
All-Star Game 39
Amar'e Stoudemire 37, 43
attitude 31, 35

Baltimore, Maryland 8, 10–11, 15, 17,
    20–21, 25, 44
Brooklyn, New York 8–9, 11

Carmelo Anthony Youth Development
    Center 44
Carmelo K. Anthony Practice Facility 43
charity 36, 43–44
Chauncey Billups 37, 44
college 17, 19, 21–23, 45

Denver Nuggets 18, 25, 27, 29, 31, 33,
    37, 39
drugs 11, 41

high school 10–15, 17, 19, 21, 25, 45

Kiyan Anthony 41
Kobe Bryant 27, 29

LeBron James 24–25, 29, 41

Mike Woodson 37, 39

NBA 9, 13, 17–19, 21, 23–25, 27, 29, 35,
    39, 41, 43, 45–46
NBA playoffs 9
New York Knicks 31, 35, 37
Nigeria 7, 9

Oak Hill Academy 18–19, 25
Olympic Games 9, 29, 41

Rookie of the Year Award 29

school 10–15, 17, 19–23, 25, 45
scouts 17, 21, 45
Syracuse Orangemen 21, 23
Syracuse University 19–23, 25, 43

Towson Catholic High School 13, 15

varsity 11–13

About the Author

Aurelia Jackson is a writer living and working in New York City. She has a passion for writing and a love of education, both of which she brings to all the work she does.

Picture Credits

Dreamstime.com:
- 6: Laurence Agron
- 8: Leo Bruce Hempell
- 10: Appalachianviews
- 12: Leungphotography
- 14: Aspenphoto
- 16: Carrienelson1
- 20: Debra Millet
- 22: Warren Rosenberg
- 24: Martin Ellis
- 28: Benkrut

- 32: Michael Flippo
- 34: Leungphotography
- 36: Carrienelson1
- 38: Leungphotography
- 40: Laurence Agron
- 42: Laurence Agron

Flickr.com:
- 18: Keith Allison
- 26: Keith Allison
- 30: Tim Shelby